D1283759

Reptiles

Chameleons

by Lyn A. Sirota

Consulting Editor: Gail Saunders-Smith, PhD
Content Consultants: Joe Maierhauser, President/CEO
Terry Phillips, Curator of Reptiles
Reptile Gardens, Rapid City, South Dakota

Capstone
press

Mankato, Minnesota

Pebble Plus is published by Capstone Press,
151 Good Counsel Drive, P.O. Box 669, Mankato, Minnesota 56002.
www.capstonepress.com

Books published by Capstone Press are manufactured with paper
containing at least 10 percent post-consumer waste.

Library of Congress Cataloging-in-Publication Data
Sirota, Lyn A., 1963–
    Chameleons / by Lyn A. Sirota.
    p. cm. — (Pebble plus. Reptiles)
    Includes bibliographical references and index.
    Summary: "Simple text and photographs present chameleons, how they look, where they live,
and what they do" — Provided by publisher.
    ISBN 978-1-4296-3320-8 (library binding : alk. paper)
    1. Chameleons — Juvenile literature. I. Title. II. Series.
QL666.L23S57 2009
597.95'6 — dc22   2009000042

Editorial Credits
Jenny Marks, editor; Matt Bruning, designer; Svetlana Zhurkin, media researcher

Photo Credits
Creatas, 9
DigitalVision, 7
Dwight R. Kuhn, 11, 17, 21
iStockphoto/Angelafoto, back cover, 1
Minden Pictures/Stephen Dalton, 15
Shutterstock/Arnaud Weisser, front cover; Sebastian Duda, 5
Visuals Unlimited/Ken Lucas, 13

Note to Parents and Teachers

The Pebble Plus Reptiles set supports science standards related to life science. This book
describes and illustrates chameleons. The images support early readers in understanding the
text. The repetition of words and phrases helps early readers learn new words. This book
also introduces early readers to subject-specific vocabulary words, which are defined in the
Glossary section. Early readers may need assistance to read some words and to use the Table of
Contents, Glossary, Read More, Internet Sites, and Index sections of the book.

Table of Contents

Busy-Eyed Lizards 4

Heat Is Neat 8

Catching Prey 12

Lizard Life 18

Glossary 22

Read More 23

Internet Sites 23

Index 24

Busy-Eyed Lizard

Chameleons are lizards

with big eyes.

They see very well.

Their bulging eyes

look everywhere.

The smallest chameleons
are only 1.4 inches
(3.6 centimeters) long.
The largest are 16 inches
(41 centimeters) long.

Heat Is Neat

Chameleons live
where the weather is warm.
Most chameleons live
on an island near Africa
called Madagascar.

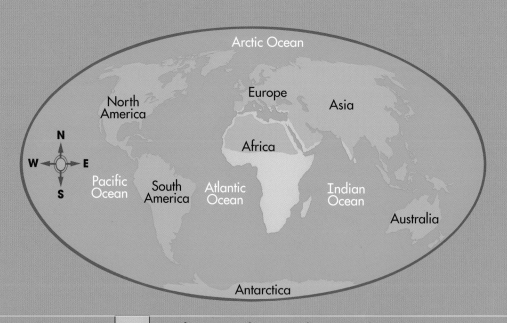

where chameleons live

When chameleons are
hot, cold, or scared,
they change color.
They also change color
to hide from predators.

Catching Prey

Chameleons hunt bugs.
Their eyes work together
to spot their prey.
One eye can look back
as the other looks forward.

A hunting chameleon

spies a tasty bug.

The chameleon flicks out

its sticky tongue.

The bug sticks to the tongue.

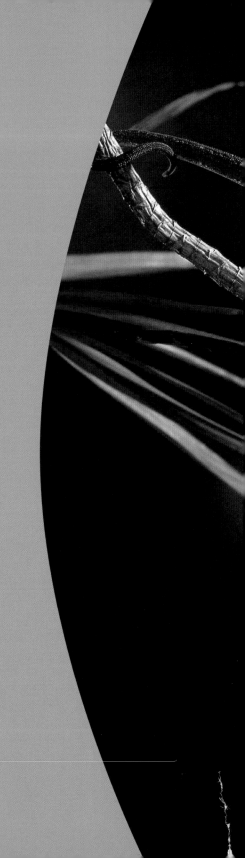

Bigger chameleons sometimes eat other lizards. Snakes and birds are food for the biggest chameleons.

Lizard Life

Female chameleons lay eggs

in tunnels they dig.

The females do not stay

to hatch their eggs.

The buried eggs are safe.

Chameleon Life Cycle

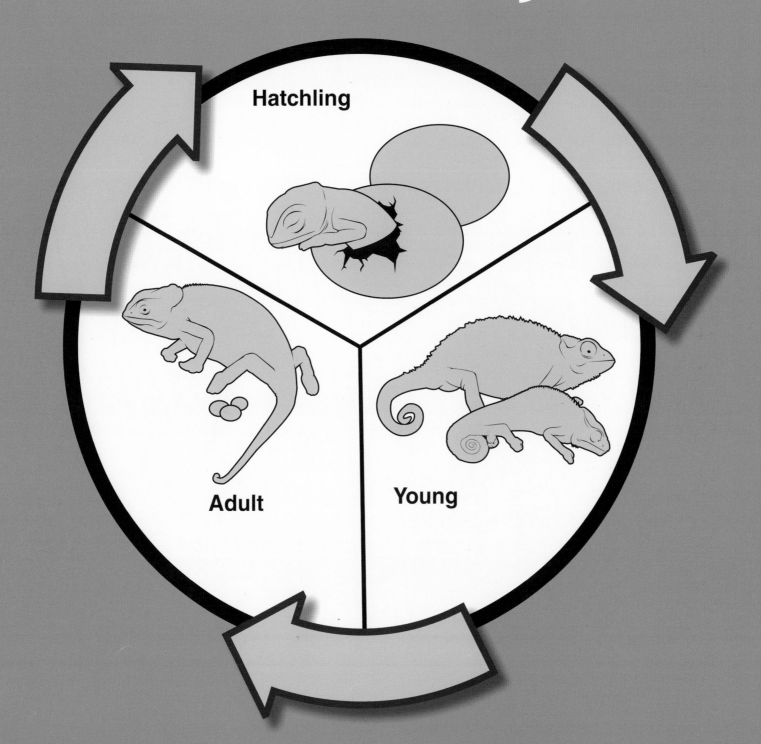

Young chameleons hatch
in 30 to 270 days.
They use an egg tooth
to break open their shells.
Hello, baby chameleons!

Glossary

bulge — to swell out like a lump

egg tooth — a toothlike part that sticks out on a chameleon's nose; the egg tooth falls off after the chameleon hatches.

lizard — a reptile with a scaly body and a long tail

Madagascar — an island near southeast Africa in the Indian Ocean

predator — an animal that hunts other animals for food

prey — an animal hunted by another animal for food

Read More

Bredeson, Carmen. *Fun Facts about Lizards!* I Like Reptiles and Amphibians! Berkeley, N.J.: Enslow Elementary, 2008.

Harrison, Paul. *Reptiles*. Up Close. New York: PowerKids Press, 2007.

LaBella, Susan. *Chameleons and Other Animals with Amazing Skin*. Scholastic News Nonfiction Readers. New York: Children's Press, 2005.

Internet Sites

FactHound offers a safe, fun way to find Internet sites related to this book. All of the sites on FactHound have been researched by our staff.

Here's all you do:

Visit *www.facthound.com*

FactHound will fetch the best sites for you!

Index

changing color, 10

digging, 18

eggs, 18, 20

egg tooth, 20

eyes, 4, 12

females, 18

hatching, 18, 20

hunting, 12, 14

Madagascar, 8

predators, 10

prey, 12, 14, 16

sight, 4

size, 6, 16

tongues, 14

young, 20

Word Count: 167

Grade: 1

Early-Intervention Level: 18